Retro Cakes
AND COOKIES

Retro Cakes

AND COOKIES

OVER 25 SWEET TREATS FROM TIMES GONE BY

WENDY SWEETSTER

CICO BOOKS

LONDON NEW YORK

Published in 2013 by CICO Books
An imprint of Ryland Peters & Small
20–21 Jockey's Fields, London WC1R 4BW
519 Broadway, 5th Floor, New York NY 10012
www.cicobooks.com

10 9 8 7 6 5 4 3 2 1

A CIP catalog record for this book is available from the
Library of Congress and the British Library.

ISBN: 978-1-908862-62-4

Printed in China

Editor: Lee Faber
Photographer: Stuart West
Stylist: Luis Peral-Aranda
Designer: Isobel Gillan

- All spoon measurements are level unless otherwise
  specified.

- Both US cup sizes or imperial and metric measurements
  have been given. Use one set of measurements only
  and not a mixture of both.

- Some of the recipes contain nuts and should not be
  consumed by anyone with a nut allergy.

- Ovens should be preheated to the specified
  temperatures. All ovens work slightly differently. We
  recommend using an oven thermometer and suggest
  you consult the maker's handbook for any special
  instructions, particularly if you are cooking in a fan-
  assisted oven, as you will need to adjust temperatures
  according to manufacturer's instructions.

- In the UK superfine (caster) sugar is most commonly
  used for making cakes, but US cooks favor granulated
  sugar, so this can be substituted if preferred.

Contents

CHAPTER ONE

Small Cakes

BARS AND BUNS

It could be a pile of tangy lemon bars, finger-licking slices of chocolate fridge cake, or pretty Maids of Honor tarts, but whatever you hand round when friends drop in for a chat, you can be sure that a plate of these small delights will disappear in seconds. They're perfect for popping into lunchboxes or picnic baskets, too.

Maids of Honor

These almond and lemon tartlets, with their crisp puff pastry crust, have been a teatime favorite in Britain since Tudor times. They are best eaten on the day they are made, but can be stored in an airtight container for 2–3 days.

Preparation time: **20 minutes**
Baking time: **15–20 minutes**
Makes 12

11oz (300g) puff pastry
Flour, for rolling out
½ cup (115g) cottage (curd) cheese
Finely grated zest of 1 lemon, plus extra for dusting
1 extra large (large UK) egg
Generous ½ cup (115g) soft light brown sugar
2 tablespoons light (single) cream
1 tablespoon milk
¾ cup (75g) ground almonds
3 tablespoons (25g) raisins
Confectioners' (icing) sugar, to dust

1 Preheat the oven to 400°F/200°C/gas mark 6.

2 Roll out the pastry very thinly on a lightly floured surface, and stamp out 12 rounds using a 3¼-inch (8-cm) plain or fluted pastry cutter, stacking the trimmings on top of each other, and re-rolling as necessary. It is important not to press the pastry trimmings together in a ball, as you'll lose the layers when the pastry bakes, and it will be tough, rather than light and flaky. Gently press each pastry circle into a 2¾-inch (7-cm) diameter cupcake pan (tin).

3 Whisk the cottage (curd) cheese, lemon zest, egg, brown sugar, cream, milk, and almonds together in a mixing bowl until evenly combined. Stir in the raisins.

4 Spoon the mixture into the pastry cases, and bake for 15–20 minutes, or until the filling is well-risen, golden brown, and feels firm to the touch. Leave the tarts to cool in the tin for 5 minutes, before carefully lifting out onto a wire rack to cool completely.

5 Dust with confectioners' (icing) sugar and a little extra lemon zest before serving.

VARIATIONS *Instead of lemon zest, the tarts could be flavored with orange zest, or a mix of the two, and the raisins replaced with dried currants, or golden raisins (sultanas).*

DID YOU KNOW?
There are various stories as to why these little cheese tarts are so named, and one legend has it that King Henry VIII dubbed them "Maids of Honor" after seeing the ladies-in-waiting attending his first queen, Catherine of Aragon, eating the sweet pastries at Richmond Palace. He was so taken with the pastries, that he imprisoned the cook, and demanded that she only bake them for guests of his choosing. She was ordered to keep the recipe secret, and reputedly even locked it up in an iron box at Richmond Palace.

Date, Apricot, and Pecan Sheet Cake

Sheet cakes are easy to make, and are ideal if you have a crowd to feed, or have been asked to make something for a school bake sale.

Preparation time: **25 minutes**
Baking time: **35–40 minutes**
Serves 15

Oil for greasing
2 sticks (225g) unsalted butter, softened
1⅛ cups (225g) superfine (caster) sugar
4 extra large (large UK) eggs
2⅔ cups (350g) self-rising flour
2 teaspoons baking powder
1 cup (150g) dried apricots, snipped into
   small pieces with scissors
1½ cups (150g) pitted (stoned) chopped dates
½ cup (50g) chopped pecans
2 tablespoons orange juice
Confectioners' (icing) sugar, to dust

1 Preheat the oven to 350°F/180°C/gas mark 4. Lightly grease a rectangular baking or roasting pan (tin) measuring approximately 11 x 8 inches (28 x 20cm), and line with baking parchment.

2 Put the butter, superfine (caster) sugar, eggs, flour, and baking powder in a mixing bowl, and beat well until all the ingredients are evenly combined. Stir in the apricots, dates, pecans, and orange juice.

3 Spoon the mixture into the pan, spreading it in an even layer, and leveling the top. Bake for 35–40 minutes, or until golden and springy to the touch. Leave to cool in the pan for 10 minutes, before turning out onto a wire rack. Peel off the lining paper, and leave to cool completely.

4 To serve, cut into 15 squares or bars, and dust with confectioners' (icing) sugar.

VARIATIONS *As well as dried fruits and nuts, you could add chocolate chips, grated lemon or orange zest, or coffee extract (essence) to the basic sponge mix. Alternatively, spoon half the mixture into the pan, and top it with a layer of very thinly sliced pears, before adding the rest of the mixture and baking.*

Lemon Bars

A crumbly shortbread base, with a sharp, tangy lemon topping, makes these teatime bars totally irresistible. Serve them topped with a generous layer of confectioners' (icing) sugar.

Preparation time: **30 minutes**
Baking time: **35–40 minutes**
Makes about 18

For the shortbread base:
Oil for greasing
1¾ cups (225g) all-purpose (plain) flour
Scant ¾ cup (115g) fine cornmeal (polenta)
2 sticks (225g) unsalted butter, diced
Generous ½ cup (115g) superfine (caster) sugar

For the lemon topping:
Scant 1 cup (175g) superfine (caster) sugar
3 extra large (large UK) eggs
½ cup (115ml) lemon juice
Finely grated zest of 2 lemons
3 tablespoons all-purpose (plain) flour
Confectioners' (icing) sugar, to dust

1 To make the shortbread, preheat the oven to 325°F/160°C/gas mark 3. Lightly grease a shallow oblong baking pan (tin) or roasting pan measuring roughly 12 x 8 inches (30 x 20cm), and line the base with baking parchment.

2 Sift the flour into a mixing bowl, and stir in the cornmeal (polenta). Rub in the butter with your fingertips, until it resembles fine breadcrumbs, and stir in the sugar, kneading the mixture lightly with your hands, so it comes together in a smooth dough.

3 Press the dough into the pan, and pat the top level with your fingers, or flatten with a spatula (palette knife), or the back of a spoon. Prick it all over with a fork and bake for 20 minutes, or until pale golden at the edges.

4 While the dough is baking, make the lemon topping. Beat the sugar and eggs together, then beat in the lemon juice and zest. Whisk in the flour until evenly combined and there are no lumps remaining.

5 Remove the shortbread from the oven, and pour the lemon mixture on top. Bake for another 15–20 minutes, or until the topping has set.

6 Leave to cool completely before turning out, and peeling off the lining paper. Cut into bars, and serve dusted with confectioners' (icing) sugar.

COOK'S TIP *If the edges of the lemon-topped shortbread become too brown during baking, trim these off with a sharp knife before cutting the remainder into bars.*

Chocolate Fridge Cake

A great recipe for getting children into the kitchen, especially if they're allowed to sample the results! This cake is very rich, so cut it into very thin slices or small bars using a small, serrated knife.

Preparation time: **20 minutes**
Chilling time: **several hours or overnight**
Serves about 20

Oil for greasing
8oz (225g) bittersweet (plain) chocolate, chopped
1 stick (115g) unsalted butter, diced
½ cup (115g) cottage (curd) cheese
½ cup (50g) walnuts, coarsely chopped
Generous ⅓ cup (75g) candied (glacé) cherries, chopped
⅔ cup (115g) golden raisins (sultanas)
1½ cups (225g) graham crackers (digestive biscuits), coarsely crushed into small pieces
1 heaped tablespoon (25g) chopped candied (mixed) peel or candied (glacé) pineapple

1 Lightly grease a 7-inch (18-cm) round or square cake pan (tin) by brushing with oil, and line the base and sides with parchment paper.

2 Put the chocolate and butter in a saucepan large enough to take all the ingredients, and melt them over very gentle heat, stirring occasionally. Allow to cool, then beat in the cottage (curd) cheese until evenly combined.

3 Stir in the chopped walnuts, cherries, golden raisins (sultanas), graham crackers (digestive biscuits), and candied (mixed) peel or candied (glacé) pineapple, until completely coated in the melted chocolate mixture.

4 Spoon into the cake pan, pressing the mixture down firmly with the back of the spoon, and smoothing the top. Press a piece of parchment paper over the surface, and cover the pan with foil.

5 Chill in the refrigerator for several hours, or overnight, until firmly set. Turn out, peel off the lining paper, and cut into thin slices, or small bars to serve.

VARIATIONS *In the US, the baked version of this type of chocolate and nut cake is known as Rocky Road. It doesn't contain fruit, and has chopped or mini marshmallows stirred into the mixture. If you like a touch of warm, sweet spice, one-third of the cherries could be replaced with chopped preserved (stem) ginger.*

COOK'S TIP *Before chopping the cherries, put them in a sieve, and rinse with hot water to remove their syrup coating. Pat the cherries dry with paper towels (kitchen paper).*

Rock Cakes

These rock cakes need no special equipment to make them, merely a baking sheet.
They are best eaten on the day they are made, and are particularly good eaten warm
from the oven, spread with butter for a special treat.

Preparation time: **15 minutes**
Baking time: **15–20 minutes**
Makes 12

Oil for greasing
1¾ cups (225g) self-rising flour
2 teaspoons baking powder
1 stick (115g) unsalted butter
6 tablespoons (75g) superfine (caster) sugar
⅜ cup (50g) raisins
⅜ cup (50g) dried currants
⅜ cup (50g) golden raisins (sultanas)
¼ teaspoon freshly grated nutmeg
1 extra large (large UK) egg
About 1 tablespoon milk
2 tablespoons turbinado (demerara) sugar

1 Preheat the oven to 400°F/200°C/gas mark 6. Lightly grease a baking sheet, and line with baking parchment.

2 Sift the flour and baking powder together in a mixing bowl, and rub in the butter until the mixture resembles fine breadcrumbs. Stir in the sugar, raisins, dried currants, golden raisins (sultanas), and nutmeg.

3 Beat together the egg and 1 tablespoon milk, and stir into the dry ingredients to make a fairly stiff mixture that leaves the sides of the bowl clean. If the mixture is too dry, add a little more milk, but it should not be too sticky.

4 Drop 12 spoonfuls of the mixture onto the baking sheet, and rough up the tops with a fork. Sprinkle with the turbinado (demerara) sugar, and bake for 15–20 minutes, or until pale golden.

5 Cool the rock cakes for 5 minutes on the baking sheet, before lifting them off with a spatula (palette knife), and transferring them to a wire rack to cool completely.

DID YOU KNOW?

Rock cakes originated in Great Britain, where they are a traditional teatime treat, but are now popular in many parts of the world. They were promoted by the Ministry of Food during the Second World War, since they require fewer eggs and less sugar than ordinary cakes; an important saving in a time of strict rationing. Traditional recipes bulked them with oatmeal, which was more readily available than white flour.

Swiss Buns

These light, finger-shaped buns with their sticky topping are irresistible eaten at
any time of day. If you really feel like indulging yourself, split them open lengthwise,
and fill them with whipped cream and strawberry jam.

Preparation time: **30 minutes (plus rising
for dough and setting for icing)**
Baking time: **10 minutes**
Makes 16

For the buns:
3¾ cups (500g) strong white bread flour,
   plus extra for kneading
1 teaspoon salt
5 teaspoons (2 × ¼-oz envelopes /2 × 7-g sachets)
   active dry yeast
½ stick (50g) unsalted butter, diced
¼ cup (50g) superfine (caster) sugar
2 extra large (large UK) eggs, beaten
Finely grated zest of 1 lemon
Scant 1¼ cups (275ml) lukewarm milk
Oil for greasing

For the icing:
1⅔ cups (225g) confectioners' (icing) sugar
3–4 tablespoons lemon juice
Pink food coloring

Sugar sprinkles, to decorate

1 To make the bun dough, sift the flour and salt into
a bowl, and stir in the yeast. Rub in the butter until it
resembles fine breadcrumbs. Stir in the sugar, eggs, lemon
zest, and milk, and mix to form a dough. Turn the dough
out onto a lightly floured surface, and knead for about
10 minutes, or until the dough is smooth and elastic,
working in a little more flour if the dough is very sticky.

2 Place the dough in an oiled bowl, cover with plastic
wrap (clingfilm), and leave to rise in a warm place for
1½–2 hours, or until doubled in size.

3 Knock the dough down, and divide it into 16 equal-
sized pieces. Roll each piece into a ball and then shape
into fingers about 4 inches (10cm) long. Place the dough
fingers on a greased baking sheet, leaving space between
them so they have room to rise.

4 Cover the baking sheet with a damp dish (tea) towel,
and leave in a warm place for 30–40 minutes, or until the
dough fingers have doubled in size, and are just touching
each other.

5 Preheat the oven to 425°F/220°C/gas mark 7, and bake
for 10 minutes until golden on top. Break the buns apart,
and transfer them to a wire rack to cool completely.

6 To make the icing, sift the confectioners' (icing) sugar
into a bowl, and stir in enough lemon juice to make a
thick spreadable icing. Dip the tops of half the buns in the
icing, smoothing the icing with a round-bladed knife. Tint
the remaining icing with a few drops of pink food coloring,
and dip the tops of the rest of the buns. Scatter the tops of
the buns with sugar sprinkles. Leave on a wire rack until
the icing has set.

Coconut Pyramids

The children will have fun helping you make and shape these sweet little cakes. What's more, the good news is that the recipe requires only a few ingredients and most cooks will already have them in their refrigerator and pantry.

Preparation time: **30 minutes (plus standing time)**
Baking time: **40–45 minutes**
Makes about 15

Oil for greasing
2 extra large (large UK) egg whites
¾ cup (150g) superfine (caster) sugar
2 cups (150g) unsweetened grated (desiccated) coconut
Pink and green food coloring (optional)

1 Lightly grease a baking sheet, and line it with baking parchment or rice paper.

2 Whisk the egg whites in a clean, grease-free bowl, until standing in stiff peaks. Gently fold in the sugar and grated (desiccated) coconut, using a large metal spoon, until evenly combined. If wished, divide the mixture between three bowls, spooning one-third into each, and tint two of them by stirring in a few drops of pink or green food coloring. Leave the mixture to stand for 15 minutes, so it has time to firm up a little.

3 Preheat the oven to 275°F/140°C/gas mark 1. With damp hands, press the mixture into small cone shapes, and place on the lined baking sheet. Bake for 40–45 minutes, or until light golden in color.

4 Transfer the pyramids to a wire rack to cool completely. They can be stored in an airtight container for up to 3 days.

COOK'S TIP *You can shape the pyramids by hand or press the mixture into an egg cup, or special pyramid mold, as you prefer.*

Butterfly Cakes

The perfect treat for a children's party, the soft sponge and creamy icing of these cakes
will appeal to junior taste buds, and they are also small enough to fit into a tiny hand.
For chocolate cakes, replace 2 tablespoons of the flour with cocoa powder.

Preparation time: **30 minutes**
Baking time: **20–25 minutes**
Makes 20 (using small paper cases)

For the cakes:
1½ sticks (175g) unsalted butter, softened
Generous ¾ cup (175g) superfine (caster) sugar
3 extra large (large UK) eggs, beaten
1 teaspoon vanilla extract (essence)
1⅓ cups (175g) self-rising flour
1 tablespoon milk

For the buttercream:
1 stick (115g) unsalted butter, softened
2 cups (225g) confectioners' (icing) sugar, sifted
2 tablespoons milk
Pastel food coloring (optional)

1 To make the cakes, preheat the oven to 350°F/180°C/
gas mark 4. Line cupcake pans (tins) with the paper cases.

2 In a mixing bowl, beat the butter until smooth, then
beat in the superfine (caster) sugar until light and creamy.
Gradually beat in the eggs, one at a time, beating well after
each addition, and adding a couple of tablespoons of the
flour to prevent the mixture from curdling.

3 Sift in the remaining flour, and stir in with the milk.
Spoon the mixture into the paper cases, and bake for about
20 minutes, or until the cakes are risen, and feel springy
to the touch. Cool in the pans for 10 minutes, before
transferring the cakes to a wire rack to cool completely.

4 To make the buttercream, beat the butter until smooth.
Gradually beat in the confectioners' (icing) sugar, and the
milk to make a smooth frosting (icing). If using food
coloring, divide the buttercream between several bowls,
and tint as required.

5 Cut a slice from the top of each cake and cut each slice
in half. Spoon or pipe the buttercream in the center of the
cakes, and press the half slices of cake into the frosting to
resemble wings.

> **COOK'S TIP** *To make chocolate buttercream, stir
> 1 tablespoon cocoa powder into 2 tablespoons hot water.
> Cool, then beat into the buttercream instead of adding milk.*

CHAPTER TWO

Cookies

AND OTHER TREATS

After a hard day, there's nothing quite like putting your feet
up and having a homemade cookie—or two—with
a reviving cup of coffee or tea. Whether it's a buttery
wedge of shortbread, a crisp snickerdoodle, or a melt-in-
the-mouth Viennese finger, no one can resist a cookie.

Snickerdoodles

These crisp cookies, dusted with cinnamon and sugar, are traditionally made with cream of tartar and baking soda (bicarbonate of soda), but a teaspoon of baking powder can be used as the raising agent instead.

Preparation time: **20 minutes**
Baking time: **10 minutes**
Makes about 30

Oil for greasing
1½ sticks (175g) unsalted butter, softened
Generous ¾ cup (175g) superfine (caster) sugar
1 extra large (large UK) egg
1 teaspoon vanilla extract
2 cups (275g) all-purpose (plain) flour, plus extra for dusting
1 teaspoon cream of tartar
½ teaspoon baking soda (bicarbonate of soda)

For coating the cookies:
1 tablespoon superfine (caster) sugar
2 teaspoons ground cinnamon

1 Preheat the oven to 400°F/200°C/gas mark 6. Lightly grease two or three baking sheets, and line them with baking parchment.

2 Beat the butter and sugar together until pale and creamy. Mix in the egg and vanilla, and then sift in the flour, cream of tartar, and baking soda (bicarbonate of soda). Stir until combined, then bring the mixture together with your hands to make a soft dough.

3 To make the coating, mix the sugar and cinnamon together on a plate. Dust your hands with flour, and pull off walnut-sized pieces of the dough. Roll these into small balls, and coat them in the cinnamon sugar.

4 Divide the balls between the baking sheets, spaced well apart so they have room to spread, and flatten them slightly. Bake for 10 minutes, or until just firm to the touch.

5 Leave the cookies to cool on the baking sheets for 5 minutes, so they have time to firm up a little, before lifting them off with a spatula (palette knife), and transferring them to a wire rack to cool completely.

DID YOU KNOW?

No one can say for sure how snickerdoodles acquired their memorable name. One claim is that they are probably German in origin, the name being a corruption of the German word "Schneckennudeln," which means "snail noodles" and is a type of pastry. Others dispute this, claiming the word was simply dreamed up by bakers in New England, who are renowned for giving their cookies quirky names.

Double Chocolate Pinwheels

Fun to look at, and even better to eat, these pinwheels would be perfect for a Fourth of July or Bonfire Night party—or any celebration that involves a firework display!

Preparation time: **30 minutes (plus chilling)**
Baking time: **12–15 minutes**
Makes about 24

Dark chocolate cookie layer:
3oz (75g) bittersweet (dark) chocolate, chopped
¾ stick (75g) unsalted butter, softened
6 tablespoons (75g) superfine (caster) sugar
1¾ cups (225g) all-purpose (plain) flour
2–3 tablespoons milk

White chocolate cookie layer:
3oz (75g) white chocolate, chopped
¾ stick (75g) unsalted butter, softened
6 tablespoons (75g) superfine (caster) sugar
1¾ cups (225g) all-purpose (plain) flour
2–3 tablespoons milk

Extra flour, for rolling
Oil for greasing

1 To make the dark chocolate layer, melt the chocolate in a bowl over a pan of hot water, stirring occasionally until smooth. Set aside to cool.

2 Beat the butter and sugar together until pale and creamy. Stir in the cooled chocolate, then sift in the flour, and beat everything together until combined. Bring the mixture together with your hands, adding enough milk to make a soft dough that is not too dry and crumbly.

3 Make up the dough for the white chocolate layer in the same way, then wrap both pieces of dough in plastic wrap (clingfilm) and chill in the fridge for 1 hour.

4 Roll out both pieces of dough on a lightly floured work surface to rectangles measuring about 15 x 10 inches (37.5 x 25cm). Carefully lift the white chocolate dough and place on top of the dark chocolate dough. Trim any rough edges neatly, and roll up like a jelly roll (Swiss roll) from one long side. If any cracks appear in the dough while you're rolling, press these back together with your fingers. Wrap the roll in plastic wrap (clingfilm) and chill again for 30 minutes.

5 Preheat the oven to 350°F/180°C/gas mark 4. Lightly grease two baking sheets, and line with baking parchment. Remove the plastic wrap (clingfilm) and, using a small sharp knife, cut the roll into about 24 slices. Place on the baking sheets and bake for about 15 minutes, or until firm to the touch. Cool on the baking sheets for 5 minutes, before transferring the cookies to a wire rack to cool completely.

COOK'S TIP *The pinwheels will spread a little as they bake, so allow some space between them when you lay them on the baking sheets.*

Melting Moments

These crisp, buttery cookies take only a moment to melt in the mouth—hence their tempting name. Candied (glacé) cherries make a colorful topping, but you can replace the cherries with blanched almonds if you prefer.

Preparation time: **20 minutes**
Baking time: **15–20 minutes**
Makes about 24

Oil for greasing
1½ sticks (175g) unsalted butter, softened
Generous ½ cup (115g) superfine (caster) sugar
1 extra large (large UK) egg
1 teaspoon vanilla extract (essence)
1⅓ cups (175g) self-rising flour
Scant ½ cup (40g) cornstarch (cornflour)
½ cup (50g) rolled oats

To decorate
6 candied (glacé) cherries, quartered

1 Preheat the oven to 375°F/190°C/gas mark 5. Grease and line two baking sheets with baking parchment.

2 Beat the butter and sugar together in a mixing bowl until light and creamy. Beat in the egg and vanilla. Sift in the self-rising flour, and the cornstarch (cornflour) and stir in.

3 Using two teaspoons, shape the mixture into 24 small balls, and roll them in the oats until coated. Place 12 on each baking sheet, and press gently with your fingers to flatten the tops slightly.

4 Top each one with a candied (glacé) cherry quarter, and bake for 15–20 minutes, or until golden. Cool on the baking sheets for 5 minutes, before transferring to a wire rack to cool completely.

COOK'S TIP *It is important to stir the flours into the creamed mixture, because if you beat them in, the baked cookies will have a tough, chewy texture. Instead of rolled oats, the balls can be rolled in shredded coconut, or crushed cornflakes, if you prefer.*

Jam Sandwich Cookies

Every child—and most grown ups too—find these jam sandwich cookies, also known as linzer sandwich cookies or Jammie Dodgers, impossible to resist. Any jam can be used, but it must be red, so you can see it clearly peeping through the hole in the top cookie.

Preparation time: **30 minutes**
Baking time: **about 10 minutes**
Makes about 20

Oil for greasing
2 sticks (225g) unsalted butter, softened
Generous ½ cup (115g) superfine (caster) sugar
2⅔ cups (350g) self-rising flour, plus extra for rolling
8–10 tablespoons raspberry, or other red jam
Confectioners' (icing) sugar, to dust

COOK'S TIP *Before sandwiching the cookies with the jam, beat the jam with a fork to loosen it and make it easier to spread.*

1 Preheat the oven to 350°F/180°C/gas mark 4. Lightly grease 3 baking sheets, and line with baking parchment, or bake in batches.

2 Beat the butter and sugar together in a mixing bowl until light and creamy. Sift in the flour, and work into the creamed mixture, pressing the mixture together with your hands, and kneading it to make a firm, smooth dough.

3 Shape the dough into a ball, and roll out on a lightly floured surface about ¼ inch (5 mm) thick. Stamp out rounds using a 2¼-inch (6-cm) fluted cookie cutter, gathering up and re-rolling trimmings, so you make a total of about 40 rounds. Using a smaller cutter, or the end of a large plain piping nozzle, cut the centers out of half the rounds.

4 Lift the rounds onto the baking sheets, allowing space for them to spread a little, and taking care not to let the rounds with holes in them become misshapen. Bake for about 10 minutes, or until golden.

5 Leave the cookies to cool on the baking sheets for 5 minutes, before lifting them off with a spatula (palette knife), and placing them on a wire rack to cool completely.

6 Sandwich the cookies together in pairs with the raspberry, or other red jam, and dust with confectioners' (icing) sugar before serving.

Shortbread Petticoat Tails

Recipes for Scottish shortbread date back to before the 12th century. During Elizabeth I's reign, shortbread started being baked in triangles that fitted together to make a circle, copying the shape of the pieces of fabric used to make a lady's petticoat. At the time, the word for pattern was "tally" so the cookies became "petticote tallis," and the name has now evolved into the petticoat tails we bake today.

Preparation time: **20 minutes**
Baking time: **40–45 minutes**
Makes 16

Oil for greasing
2 sticks (225g) unsalted butter, softened
Generous ½ cup (115g) superfine (caster) sugar
1¾ cups (225g) all-purpose (plain) flour, plus extra
   for dusting
Generous ¾ cup (100g) rice flour
Extra superfine (caster) sugar, for dredging

1 Preheat the oven to 300°F/150°C/gas mark 2. Lightly grease two 7-inch (18-cm) layer cake pans (sandwich tins), and line the base of each with a disc of baking parchment.

2 In a mixing bowl, beat the butter and sugar together until pale and creamy. Sift in the all-purpose (plain) flour and rice flour, and stir until just mixed in.

3 Bring the mixture together with floured hands, then divide it between the pans, pressing it down in an even layer. Prick the tops with a fork to prevent the shortbread rising in the middle, and mark the edges with the back of the fork or your fingers, to make a fluted pattern. Bake for 40–45 minutes, or until the shortbread is pale golden.

4 Dredge the top with superfine (caster) sugar and cut each round into 8 triangles. Leave in the pans for 10 minutes to firm up, before carefully removing to a wire rack to cool completely.

COOK'S TIP *To ensure the shortbread is light and crisp, and melts in your mouth, it is important not to overwork the dough, whether you make it by hand or pulse the ingredients together in a food processor. Simply press it together gently with your fingers, rather than kneading it like bread, and work in a cool atmosphere. Shortbread originates in Scotland where Highland kitchens are notoriously cold—which is maybe the secret of its success north of the Border!*

Ginger Nuts

Also called gingersnaps, recipes for spicy cookies like these are popular all around the world, particularly in Scandinavia, where, in addition to the spices used here, freshly ground black pepper is added to the dough for an extra kick.

Preparation time: **25 minutes**
Baking time: **15 minutes**
Makes 18

Oil for greasing
1 scant cup (115g) all-purpose (plain) flour
1 teaspoon baking powder
1 teaspoon baking soda (bicarbonate of soda)
1½ teaspoons ground ginger
½ teaspoon ground cinnamon
¼ teaspoon freshly grated nutmeg
½ stick (50g) unsalted butter, diced
¼ cup (50g) soft dark brown (muscovado) sugar
1½ tablespoons golden syrup, or light corn syrup
About ¼ cup (50g) superfine (caster) sugar, for coating

1 Preheat the oven to 350°F/180°C/gas mark 4. Lightly grease two or three baking sheets, and line them with baking parchment.

2 Sift the flour, baking powder, baking soda (bicarbonate of soda), ginger, cinnamon, and nutmeg into a mixing bowl. Add the butter, and rub it in with your fingertips until the mixture resembles fine breadcrumbs. Break up any lumps in the brown sugar with the back of a spoon, or your fingers, and stir in.

3 If using golden syrup, which is very thick, warm it in a saucepan over low heat, or in a small non-metal bowl in the microwave, until it is runny, but not boiling hot. (Corn syrup has a runnier consistency and does not need to be warmed.) Pour the syrup into the other ingredients. Stir to mix it in, then bring the dough together with your hands until it forms a soft ball.

4 Cut the dough into 18 equal-sized pieces, and roll each piece into a ball. Spread out the superfine (caster) sugar on a plate, and roll the balls of dough in the sugar until they are evenly coated. Divide the balls between the baking sheets, spaced well apart, so they have room to spread, and flatten each with your hand, or the bottom of a glass.

5 Bake in the oven for 15 minutes, or until just firm. Cool the ginger nuts on the baking sheets for 5 minutes, before transferring them to a wire rack to cool completely.

COOK'S TIP *To ensure the ginger nuts don't lose their freshly baked crunch, store them in an airtight container as soon as they have cooled completely.*

Chocolate-Dipped Viennese Fingers

Similar to shortbread, but lighter and crumblier, these chocolate-dipped cookies are the perfect accompaniment to coffee or tea. They can also be served with desserts, as an accompaniment to mousses, ice cream, and fruit salads.

Preparation time: **15 minutes**
Baking time: **7–8 minutes**
Makes about 20

For the cookie dough:

1 stick + 2 teaspoons (125g) unsalted butter, softened
3½ tablespoons (25g) confectioners' (icing) sugar, sifted
½ teaspoon vanilla extract (essence)
¼ teaspoon baking powder
1 scant cup (115g) all-purpose (plain) flour
Scant ½ cup (40g) cornstarch (cornflour)
About 2 tablespoons milk

For the chocolate icing:

3½ oz (100g) bittersweet (dark) or milk chocolate

1 Preheat the oven to 325°F/160°C/gas mark 3. Make the cookie dough: in a mixing bowl, beat the butter until soft and creamy. Sift in the confectioners' (icing) sugar, add the vanilla, and beat again until the mixture is light and fluffy.

2 Sift in the baking powder, all-purpose (plain) flour and cornstarch (cornflour), and add the milk. Stir, rather than beat, everything together to make a smooth, soft dough.

3 Line two baking sheets with baking parchment. Spoon the mixture into a piping bag fitted with a large star nozzle. Pipe the mixture onto the baking sheets in lines about 4 inches (10cm) long, spaced well apart, to make about 20 cookies.

4 Bake in the oven for 7–8 minutes, or until the cookies are pale golden. Leave to cool on the baking sheets for 5 minutes, before very carefully transferring to a wire rack with a spatula (palette knife) to cool completely.

5 To make the chocolate icing, break or chop the chocolate into small pieces, and place in a heatproof bowl. Stand the bowl over a pan of simmering water, making sure the bottom of the bowl does not touch the water, and leave until the chocolate has melted, stirring occasionally until smooth.

6 Re-line the baking sheets with clean baking parchment or foil. Dip both ends of the cookies into the melted chocolate, let the excess chocolate drip back into the bowl, and place the cookies back on the baking sheets until the chocolate has set. When set, store the cookies in an airtight container.

COOK'S TIPS *The mixture needs to be soft enough to pipe, but it must also be firm enough to hold its shape, so you may need to adjust the quantity of milk to ensure the right consistency. The baked cookies are crumbly and delicate, so handle them with care, as you could break them when lifting them off the baking sheets and dipping them in chocolate if you're too heavy-handed. On the other hand, eating the broken ones is the cook's perk!*

Macaroons

Not to be confused with French *macarons*—those delicate rainbow-hued cookies sandwiched with cream, that you see packed into pretty boxes in French pâtisserie shops— English macaroons are chunkier, chewier, and easier to make.

Preparation time: **20 minutes**
Baking time: **20–25 minutes**
Makes 10

Oil for greasing
1 extra large (large UK) egg white, plus extra for glazing
½ cup (50g) ground almonds
½ cup (100g) superfine (caster) sugar
1 tablespoon ground rice
½ teaspoon almond extract (essence)
10 whole blanched almonds or 5 whole almonds split in half

1 Lightly grease a baking sheet, and line it with rice paper or baking parchment. Preheat the oven to 350°F/ 180°C/gas mark 4.

2 Whisk the egg white in a clean, grease-free bowl until standing in stiff peaks. Gently fold in the ground almonds, sugar, ground rice, and almond extract using a large metal spoon.

3 Place 10 spoonfuls of the mixture onto the baking sheet, leaving plenty of room for the macaroons to spread. Top each with a whole or split almond. Beat the egg white for glazing with a fork to break it up, and brush over the macaroons.

4 Bake in the oven for 20–25 minutes, or until golden. Transfer the macaroons to a wire rack to cool, and store in an airtight container when completely cool.

VARIATIONS *To make American Coconut Macaroons, use 2 extra-large (large UK) egg whites, and reduce the quantity of ground almonds to ¼ cup (25g). Make up the mixture as before, folding 2⅔ cups (200g) shredded (flaked) coconut into the whisked whites with the almonds, sugar, ground rice, and almond extract. Coconut macaroons should have a moist texture, so it's important to use shredded coconut (available from supermarkets and Asian food stores), rather than desiccated coconut, which would make the mixture too dry.*

CHAPTER THREE

Large Cakes

A homemade cake given as a gift to a special friend beats
a box of chocolates or a bunch of flowers every time.
A coffee-walnut layer cake layered with soft, sweet
buttercream or a devil's food cake frosted with the darkest
chocolate are totally indulgent treats, but a simple iced
orange seed cake or cherry-almond sponge is equally
special. Just one bite will fill you with nostalgia and remind
you of your favorite cakes when you were young.

Coffee-Walnut Layer Cake

A sumptuous, totally indulgent cake that is perfect for a family get-together. Standing proudly on a cake stand, coated with a generous layer of buttercream and walnut halves, nobody will be able to resist coming back for a second slice!

Preparation time: **30 minutes**
Baking time: **25–30 minutes**
Serves 12

For the cake:
Oil for greasing
2 sticks (225g) unsalted butter, softened
1⅛ cups (225g) superfine (caster) sugar
4 extra large (large UK) eggs
1¾ cups (225g) self-rising flour
2 teaspoons baking powder
1 tablespoon instant coffee dissolved in 2 tablespoons
  hot water, and cooled
1 cup (115g) chopped walnuts

For the buttercream:
1½ sticks (175g) unsalted butter
2½ cups (350g) confectioners' (icing) sugar
1 tablespoon instant coffee dissolved in 2 tablespoons
  hot water, and cooled
Walnut halves, to decorate

> **COOK'S TIP** *Before making the cake, leave the butter at room temperature for several hours, so it has time to soften. If using straight from the fridge, cut it into small pieces, and microwave it in a non-metal mixing bowl on defrost power for about 1 minute. The butter needs to be very soft and creamy—but not melted—so it combines easily with the other ingredients.*

1 To make the cake, preheat the oven to 325°F/160°C/gas mark 3. Lightly grease three 8-inch (20-cm) layer cake pans (sandwich tins), and line the bases with baking parchment.

2 Put the butter, sugar, eggs, self-rising flour, baking powder, and dissolved coffee in a large mixing bowl, and beat together using an electric hand mixer on low speed, or a wooden spoon, until smooth. Stir in the chopped walnuts.

3 Divide the mixture between the pans, spreading it in even layers and leveling the tops. Bake for 25–30 minutes, or until risen and springy to the touch. Leave the cakes to cool in the pans for 5 minutes, before turning out onto a wire rack to cool completely.

4 To make the buttercream, beat the butter until soft and creamy. Gradually sift in the confectioners' (icing) sugar, beating well after each addition, and adding the dissolved coffee after three quarters of the sugar has been added.

5 Sandwich the cake layers with some of the buttercream, and spread the remainder on top. Decorate with a ring of walnut halves.

Devil's Food Cake

This has been a fixture in every American baker's repertoire since the first Devil's Food Cake recipe was published in 1905. Dark and wickedly delicious, this is a big cake for a big occasion, such as a special birthday or an engagement party.

Preparation time: **45 minutes**
Baking time: **about 35 minutes**
Serves 16–20

For the cake:
Oil for greasing
3½ oz (100g) bittersweet (dark) chocolate, chopped
¾ cup (175ml) cold water
1½ sticks (175g) unsalted butter, softened
1½ cups (300g) soft dark brown (muscovado) sugar
3 extra large (large UK) eggs, beaten
2¼ cups (300g) all-purpose (plain) flour
¾ cup (175ml) sour cream
1 teaspoon vanilla extract (essence)
1½ teaspoons baking soda (bicarbonate of soda)

For the frosting (icing):
⅔ cup (150ml) water
¼ cup (50g) soft dark brown (muscovado) sugar
2¼ sticks (250g) unsalted butter, diced
14oz (400g) bittersweet (dark) chocolate, chopped
Extra grated bittersweet (dark) chocolate, to decorate

1 Preheat the oven to 375°F/190°C/gas mark 5. Lightly grease three 8-inch (20-cm) layer cake pans (sandwich tins) and line the bases with baking parchment.

2 To make the cake, put the chocolate and water in a heavy-based pan, and heat gently until the chocolate melts, stirring until smooth.

3 Beat the butter in a mixing bowl until creamy, then gradually beat in the brown sugar. Add the eggs one at a time, beating well after each addition, and adding a tablespoon of the flour to prevent the mixture from curdling. Stir in the melted chocolate.

4 Mix together the sour cream and vanilla, and sift the rest of the flour with the baking soda (bicarbonate of soda). Stir the sour cream into the chocolate mixture alternately with the flour, until all the ingredients are evenly combined.

5 Divide the mixture between the three pans, spreading it in even layers and leveling the tops. Bake for 25 minutes, or until the sponge layers feel springy to the touch. Cool in the pans for 10 minutes, before turning out onto a wire rack to cool completely, and removing the lining paper.

6 To make the frosting (icing), put the water, sugar, and butter into a heavy-based pan, and heat gently until the sugar dissolves, and the butter has melted. Add the chopped chocolate, and stir constantly over very low heat until smooth, taking care not to let the chocolate stick to the bottom of the pan and burn. Transfer the frosting to a bowl, and leave in a cool place until it is thick enough to spread.

7 Spread a layer of frosting over two of the cake layers, and sandwich all three together. Spread the rest of the frosting over the top and sides of the cake, and decorate with a dusting of grated dark chocolate.

Dundee Cake

Lighter than many traditional heavy fruit cakes, similar cakes to this are baked all over Scotland—and in many other places as well—not just Dundee. The topping of whole almonds gives the cake an attractive finish, without the need to add layers of marzipan and royal icing.

Preparation time: **30 minutes**
Baking time: **about 1¾ hours**
Serves 8–10

Oil for greasing
2 sticks (225g) unsalted butter, softened
1⅛ cups (225g) superfine (caster) sugar
Finely grated zest of 1 orange
4 extra large (large UK) eggs
1¾ cups (225g) all-purpose (plain) flour
1½ teaspoons baking powder
1 teaspoon ground cinnamon
½ cup (50g) ground almonds
2¼ cups (350g) mixed dried fruit
⅜ cup (50g) chopped candied (mixed) peel
1 tablespoon whisky, milk, or orange juice
⅜ cup (50g) whole blanched almonds

1 Preheat the oven to 300°F/150°C/gas mark 2. Lightly grease an 8-inch (20-cm) deep round cake pan (tin), and line the base and sides with baking parchment.

2 Beat the butter and sugar together in a mixing bowl until light and creamy. Beat in the orange zest, and then the eggs, one at a time, adding a tablespoon of the flour with each egg to prevent the mixture from curdling.

3 Sift in the rest of the flour with the baking powder and ground cinnamon, and stir in with the ground almonds. Finally stir in the dried fruit, candied (mixed) peel, and whisky, milk, or orange juice.

4 Spoon the mixture into the pan, spreading it in an even layer and leveling the top, and arrange the whole almonds on top in concentric circles. Bake for about 1¾ hours, or until a toothpick pushed into the center of the cake comes out clean.

5 Leave the cake to cool completely before removing it from the pan.

DID YOU KNOW?

Despite some fanciful food historians claiming Dundee cake was created for Mary Queen of Scots, the recipe most likely dates from the mid 19th century, and the Keiller marmalade company. Founded in 1797 by James Keiller and his mother Janet in the Scottish city of Dundee, it is believed the company began producing Dundee cakes as a by-product of the marmalade making process.

Pineapple Upside-Down Cake

A layer of honeyed pineapple rings and candied (glacé) cherries is arranged over the base of the pan (tin) before the sponge layer is spread on top, and the cake baked until it is light and golden. This cake is equally good served hot with custard, or cold with Greek yogurt or ice cream.

Preparation time: **20 minutes**
Baking time: **40–45 minutes**
Serves 6–8

Oil for greasing
4 tablespoons clear honey
6 candied (glacé) cherries
4–5 pineapple rings, canned or fresh
1 stick + 1 tablespoon (125g) unsalted butter, softened
Scant ⅔ cup (125g) superfine (caster) sugar
2 extra large (large UK) eggs, beaten
Generous 1 cup (150g) self-rising flour
1 teaspoon ground ginger

1 Preheat the oven to 350°F/180°C/gas mark 4. Lightly grease a 7-inch (19-cm) round cake pan (tin), and line the base and sides with baking parchment.

2 Warm the honey, and pour it over the base of the cake pan. Put the candied (glacé) cherries in a sieve, and run hot water over them to rinse off their syrup coating. Pat the cherries dry with paper towels (kitchen paper) and cut each one in half. Arrange a whole pineapple slice in the center of the pan, and the other slices around it, cutting them to fit as necessary. Place a cherry half (cut side up) in the middle of the center ring, and tuck the rest in the gaps between the pineapple rings.

3 In a mixing bowl, beat together the butter and sugar until light and creamy. Gradually beat in the eggs, one at a time, adding a tablespoon of the flour to prevent the mixture from curdling. Sift in the remaining flour, and stir in with the ginger.

4 Spoon the mixture over the pineapple and cherries, spreading it in an even layer, and leveling the top. Bake for 40–45 minutes, or until just firm to the touch, and the sponge springs back when lightly pressed.

5 Cool the cake in the pan for 5 minutes, before turning it out onto a serving plate, and peeling off the lining paper. Serve hot or cold.

COOK'S TIPS *When spreading the sponge mixture into the cake pan, take care not to dislodge any pieces of fruit, or your carefully arranged pattern of pineapple rings and cherries will be lost when you turn the cake out. If you're serving the cake cold, you can give the fruit an extra shine, by brushing the pineapple slices with a little warmed apricot jam.*

Christmas Yule Log

An irresistible alternative to a heavy fruit cake for the festive season. Decorations can be simple, such as sprigs of holly made from marzipan or sugarpaste, or get the children to help you add robins, marzipan pine cones, meringue mushrooms, and maybe even a small snowman.

Preparation time: **45 minutes**
Baking time: **20 minutes**
Serves 8–10

For the cake:
Oil for greasing
6 extra large (large UK) eggs, separated
¾ cup (150g) superfine (caster) sugar
1 teaspoon vanilla extract (essence)
½ cup (50g) cocoa powder

For the filling:
1¼ cups (300ml) heavy (double) cream
3 tablespoons confectioners' (icing) sugar

For the chocolate frosting (icing):
8oz (225g) bittersweet (dark) chocolate, chopped
1 cup (225ml) heavy (double) cream

To decorate:
Marzipan or sugarpaste holly leaves and berries

1 Preheat the oven to 350°F/180°C/gas mark 4. Lightly grease a 13 x 9-inch (33 x 23-cm) jelly roll pan (Swiss roll tin) and line with baking parchment.

2 To make the cake, put the egg yolks and sugar in a mixing bowl, and whisk until pale, thick, and creamy. Whisk in the vanilla, then sift in the cocoa powder, and fold in until evenly combined.

3 Whisk the egg whites in a clean, grease-free bowl, until standing in stiff peaks. Stir 1 tablespoon into the chocolate mixture to loosen it, before carefully folding in the remainder with a large metal spoon. It is important that there are no lumps of egg white left in the mixture, as these will prevent the sponge from baking evenly.

4 Pour the mixture into the pan, spreading it into the corners, and bake for 20 minutes, or until risen, and just firm to the touch. Turn out onto a sheet of clean baking parchment, remove the lining paper, and roll up from one short side with the parchment inside. Lift onto a wire rack and leave to cool completely.

5 To make the filling, whip the cream with the confectioners' (icing) sugar until thick. Unroll the sponge, and spread the cream over it to within ½ inch (1cm) of the edges, reserving a little cream to neaten the ends. Roll up again from one short side, and pipe or spread a swirl of cream to fill any gaps at each end.

6 To make the frosting (icing), put the chocolate in a bowl. Heat the cream in a heavy-based pan and as soon as it comes to a boil, pour it over the chocolate in the bowl. Leave until the chocolate has melted, then whisk or stir until smooth. Allow the frosting to cool and thicken, stirring occasionally.

7 Cover the log with the frosting, roughing it up to resemble tree bark, then decorate with marzipan or sugarpaste holly leaves and berries.

Iced Orange Seed Cake

As with pound cake (see page 58), recipes for seed cake date from Victorian times. Early recipes always used caraway as the "seed," partly for its sharp aniseed flavor, but also because it aided digestion. If you find caraway too harsh, you could use poppy seeds or fennel seeds instead.

Preparation time: **25 minutes**
Baking time: **45–50 minutes**
Serves 8

Oil for greasing
1½ sticks (175g) unsalted butter, softened
Scant cup (175g) unrefined superfine sugar
　(golden caster sugar)
Finely grated zest of 1 orange
1 tablespoon caraway or fennel seeds
2 extra large (large UK) eggs, separated
1⅓ cups (175g) self-rising flour
½ cup (50g) ground almonds
¼ teaspoon freshly grated nutmeg
2 tablespoons milk

For the icing:
½ cup (75g) confectioners' (icing) sugar
About 2 tablespoons orange juice
Orange food coloring

To decorate *(see Cook's Tip)*:
Candied (crystallized) orange peel
Additional superfine (caster) sugar

1 Preheat the oven to 350°F/180°C/gas mark 4. Lightly grease a 9 x 5 x 3-inch (900-g) loaf pan (tin), and line the base and sides with baking parchment.

2 Beat the butter and sugar together until pale and creamy. Stir in the grated orange zest, and caraway or fennel seeds, followed by the egg yolks, one at a time.

3 Sift in the flour, and stir in with the ground almonds, nutmeg, and milk. Whisk the egg whites in a clean, grease-free bowl, until standing in firm peaks. Stir one tablespoon of the whites into the mixture to loosen it, then gently fold in the remainder using a large metal spoon.

4 Spoon the mixture into the pan, spreading it in an even layer and leveling the top, and bake for 45–50 minutes, or until a toothpick pushed into the center of the cake comes out clean. Leave to cool in the pan for 30 minutes before turning out onto a wire rack to cool completely.

5 To make the icing, sift the confectioners' (icing) sugar into a bowl, and stir in enough orange juice to make a paste thick enough to coat the back of a spoon. Tint with a little orange food coloring, and drizzle or spread the icing over the cake. Decorate with candied (crystallized) orange peel, and leave until the icing has set.

COOK'S TIP *To make candied (crystallized) orange peel, pare strips of peel from an orange using a vegetable peeler, taking care not to remove too much pith with the peel. Cut the strips into fine long shreds with a small sharp knife. Heat a generous ½ cup (115g) granulated or superfine (caster) sugar in ½ cup (100ml) water, and, once the sugar has dissolved, add the orange peel. Simmer for 10–15 minutes, or until the peel becomes transparent. Drain well, and, using two forks, toss the peel in superfine (caster) sugar until coated. Leave to cool before using to decorate the cake.*

Cherry-Almond Sponge

A cake that's easy to make, and that the whole family will love. Stand it on a pretty plate, and watch it disappear like magic as soon as you put it on the table.

Preparation time: **20 minutes**
Baking time: **1–1¼ hours**
Serves 8

1¾ cups (225g) candied (glacé) cherries
1⅓ cups (175g) self-rising flour
Oil for greasing
1½ sticks (175g) unsalted butter, softened
Generous ¾ cup (175g) superfine (caster) sugar
3 extra large (large UK) eggs
1 teaspoon vanilla extract (essence)
1 generous cup (115g) ground almonds
2 tablespoons milk
3 tablespoons slivered (flaked) almonds

1 Rinse the syrup off the cherries by putting them in a sieve and running hot water over them. Drain and pat the cherries dry with paper towels (kitchen paper). Cut into quarters, and toss them in a tablespoon of the flour.

2 Preheat the oven to 325°F/160°C/gas mark 3. Lightly grease an 8-inch (20-cm) deep round cake pan (tin), and line the base and sides with baking parchment.

3 Beat the butter and sugar together until light and creamy. Mix the eggs and vanilla together, and beat into the creamed mixture a little at a time, beating well after each addition, and adding a tablespoon of the flour to prevent the mixture from curdling. Sift in the rest of the flour, and stir in with the ground almonds, candied (glacé) cherries, and milk.

4 Spoon the mixture into the cake pan, spreading it in an even layer and leveling the top. Scatter over the slivered (flaked) almonds. Bake the cake in the oven for 1–1¼ hours, or until a toothpick pushed into the center of the cake comes out clean. Cool the cake in the pan for 30 minutes, before turning it out onto a wire rack to cool completely.

COOK'S TIP *Rinsing the syrup off the cherries, and dusting them with a little flour, helps prevent them sinking to the bottom of the cake during baking.*

Pound Cake

This cake makes an excellent dessert served warm or cold. If serving cold, cut into slices, and accompany with strawberries or raspberries, and whipped cream or Greek yogurt. If serving warm, a red fruit compote of summer berries or plums makes a good accompaniment.

Preparation time: **25 minutes**
Baking time: **1 hour**
Serves 12

Oil for greasing
2 sticks (225g) unsalted butter, softened
1¼ cups (250g) superfine (caster) sugar
5 extra large (large UK) eggs
1 teaspoon vanilla extract (essence)
3 cups (400g) self-rising flour
1 cup (225ml) buttermilk
2 tablespoons nib, hail, or pearl sugar,
   or crushed sugar cubes

1 Preheat the oven to 325°F/160°C/gas mark 3. Lightly grease an 8-inch (20-cm) deep square cake pan (tin), and line the base and sides with baking parchment.

2 In a large mixing bowl, beat the butter until soft and creamy, then gradually beat in the superfine (caster) sugar. Lightly whisk the eggs and vanilla together, and beat into the creamed mixture, adding a tablespoon of the flour to prevent it curdling.

3 Stir in the rest of the flour, alternately with the buttermilk, until evenly combined.

4 Spoon the mixture into the pan, spreading it in an even layer, and leveling the top, and sprinkle over the nib sugar. Bake for about 1 hour, or until the cake is firm to the touch, golden brown, and is starting to shrink from the sides of the pan.

5 Cool in the pan for 30 minutes, before turning out onto a wire rack to cool completely.

DID YOU KNOW?

When Queen Victoria was on the throne, bakers made cakes that were much larger than they are today, measuring their ingredients in one-pound quantities, which was how the pound cake got its name. Today we think of pound cake as being a buttery, sweet, all-American favorite, but modern recipes, like those of the British equivalent, Madeira cake, owe their provenance to those Victorian bakers.

Spiced Apple Cake

Wherever there are orchards, you'll find recipes for apple cakes; some plain, some spicy, some crunchy with nuts, and every cook will claim hers is the best. This recipe would be good served cold at a potluck, church supper, or county (village) fair. Alternatively, serve warm from the oven as a dessert.

Preparation time: **30 minutes**
Baking time: **1½–1¾ hours**
Serves 12

Oil for greasing
14oz (400g) (about 3 medium) cooking apples,
   such as Granny Smith
2 tablespoons lemon juice
2 sticks (225g) unsalted butter, diced and softened
1⅛ cups (225g) soft light brown sugar
Finely grated zest of 1 lemon
4 extra large (large UK) eggs
2⅔ cups (350g) self-rising flour
2 teaspoons baking powder
1 teaspoon ground cinnamon
½ teaspoon freshly grated nutmeg
½ teaspoon allspice
1 cup (115g) chopped walnuts
Generous ¾ cup (115g) golden raisins (sultanas)
2 tablespoons apricot jam

1 Preheat the oven to 350°F/180°C/gas mark 4. Lightly grease a 9-inch (23-cm) deep round cake pan (tin), and line the base and sides with baking parchment.

2 Peel, core, and cut the apples into thin slices. Put them on a large plate, sprinkle the lemon juice over them, and set aside.

3 Put the butter, brown sugar, lemon zest, eggs, flour, baking powder, cinnamon, nutmeg, and allspice in a large mixing bowl, and beat together until smooth. Stir in the walnuts and golden raisins (sultanas).

4 Spoon half the cake mixture into the pan, spreading it in an even layer and leveling the top. Arrange half the apple slices on top, followed by the remaining cake mixture, and finally the rest of the apple slices.

5 Bake in the oven for 1½–1¾ hours, or until a toothpick pushed into the center of the cake comes out clean. Once the apples on top have browned enough, cover the top of the cake with a sheet of foil to prevent them browning any more.

6 Leave the cake to cool in the pan for 20 minutes, before turning it out onto a wire rack and removing the lining paper. Warm the apricot jam and brush over the top of the cake. Serve warm or cold on its own, or with a scoop of whipped cream, or ice cream.

COOK'S TIP *If Granny Smiths are not available, choose another variety of apple that is recommended for cooking. Cooking apples should have a tart flavor, and crunchy, firm flesh.*

Cornish Saffron Cake

In medieval times, saffron was a popular flavoring; its delicate strands giving doughs a rich golden hue. In England at that time, saffron was grown in Cornwall, where it was added to cakes made for special occasions. Saffron cakes and buns are still baked there today, the traditional accompaniment being locally-produced clotted cream. Americans have adopted this cake, calling it a "bread."

Preparation time: **45 minutes (plus soaking time for saffron and rising time for dough)**
Baking time: **about 50 minutes**
Makes one 9 × 5 × 3-inch (900-g) loaf cake

1 teaspoon saffron strands
2 tablespoons hot water
3¼ cups (450g) strong white bread flour, plus extra for kneading
½ teaspoon salt
5 teaspoons (2 × ¼-oz envelopes/2 × 7-g sachets) active dry yeast
1¼ sticks (150g) unsalted butter, diced
¼ cup (50g) unrefined superfine (golden caster) sugar
1½ cups (200g) dried currants
⅜ cup (50g) chopped candied (mixed) peel
1 teaspoon ground cinnamon
½ teaspoon ground allspice
¼ teaspoon freshly grated nutmeg
2 extra large (large UK) eggs
½ cup (115ml) lukewarm milk
Oil for greasing

To glaze:
2 tablespoons (25g) unsalted butter, melted
2 tablespoons (25g) unrefined superfine (golden caster) sugar

1 Crumble the saffron strands into a small bowl, and add the hot water. Leave to soak for 30 minutes.

2 Sift the flour and salt into a mixing bowl, and stir in the yeast. Rub in the butter until the mixture resembles fine breadcrumbs. Stir in the sugar, dried currants, candied (mixed) peel, cinnamon, allspice, and nutmeg.

3 Beat together the eggs and milk, and add to the dry ingredients with the saffron and its soaking water. Stir to mix, then work everything together to make a dough. Transfer the dough to a lightly floured board, and knead for about 10 minutes, or until it is smooth and elastic.

4 Put the dough in a lightly greased bowl, cover with plastic wrap (clingfilm), and leave in a warm place for 3–4 hours, or until doubled in size.

5 Grease a 9 × 5 × 3-inch (900-g) loaf pan (tin), or line with a parchment paper case. Knock the dough down, knead for 1–2 minutes, and then shape into a loaf. Put the dough in the pan, seam side down, cover with a damp dish (tea) towel, and leave to rise again for about 2 hours in a warm place, until the dough rises to the top of the pan.

6 Preheat the oven to 400°F/200°C/gas mark 6, and bake for 20 minutes. Reduce the oven temperature to 350°F/180°C/gas mark 4, and bake for another 25–30 minutes, or until the base of the loaf sounds hollow when tapped. Glaze the top of the loaf by brushing with the melted butter, and sprinkling over the sugar. Bake for an additional 3 minutes. Turn the loaf out onto a wire rack to cool, and serve cut into slices, spread with butter, or clotted cream and jam.

Index